Men's Konkatsu Tales

I Talk You Talk Press

CONTENTS

INTRODUCTION

"Konkatsu" is a Japanese word.

It means "searching for a marriage partner".

We asked many of our male friends in Japan about their search for a marriage partner.

The men told us some very interesting stories. We chose eight of these stories for this book.

In this book, there are some Japanese words.

The Japanese words are:

1. *o-miai* - an introductory meeting / a formal marriage interview
2. *Mt. Daisen* - a mountain in West Japan
3. *Izakaya* - a Japanese pub/restaurant
4. *san* - Mr/Ms

ONE

H san (36) Tottori Prefecture

Two years ago, I wanted to get married. However, in my town, there were not many young women. There were some women in my office, but they were already married.

I worked hard every day, so I didn't have the chance to meet a marriage partner. Also, I am very shy. It is difficult for me to talk to women. So, my mother arranged a traditional *o-miai* introduction meeting. The go-between was my mother's cousin. The woman was the daughter of my mother's cousin's friend.

We met at a restaurant in Yonago City. My mother, my mother's cousin and the girl's mother came to the meeting. I was very nervous. I was the only man! The woman was thirty-three. Her name was Sachiko. She was very beautiful. She was also very shy.

My mother and Sachiko's mother talked a lot. I wanted to talk to Sachiko, but I was too shy. So, we ate a lot of delicious food, but we didn't talk. After lunch, my mother's cousin said, "The weather is nice today. Take Sachiko for a drive to Mt. Daisen."

So, Sachiko and I went for a drive. I was very nervous. We drove to Mt. Daisen. She said, "Mt. Daisen looks so beautiful today!"

I said, "Yes, it does."

She said, "Do you often drive to Mt. Daisen?"

I said, "No, I don't. But I come here in winter. I like skiing and snowboarding."

She said, "Oh really? I like snowboarding, too!"

We talked about snowboarding.

She said, "Did you go snowboarding last winter?"

I said, "Yes, I did. I went to Mt. Daisen every Sunday morning in January."

She said, "Really? So did I! I went snowboarding at Mt. Daisen every Sunday morning in January and February!"

We laughed. After that, we talked a lot. I enjoyed the day very much.

When I got home, I talked to my mother.

I said, "Mother, I want to see Sachiko again."

My mother was very pleased and quickly called her cousin to tell her the news.

Sachiko also enjoyed the day. She wanted to see me again!

So, two weeks later, I met Sachiko again. We went to the movie theater. After that, we went to a family restaurant and talked.

A year later, Sachiko and I got married.

I like Sachiko because she is a very interesting person. She is very kind, and we have the same hobby. I am very shy, so talking is difficult for me. But with Sachiko, I can talk about many things. We are very happy together.

TWO

A san (26) Izumo area, Shimane Prefecture

I had a girlfriend, but we broke up last year. I was disappointed. I wanted a new girlfriend.

I asked my friend for advice.

He said, "There is a single woman in my office. She is twenty-four and she is very cute. Shall I introduce you to her?"

I said, "Yes, please!"

So, my friend arranged a small party at an *izakaya*. My friend, another friend, the woman, her two friends and I went to the party. The woman was very cute. Her nail art was very pretty and she wore a lot of make-up. Her friends were very cute, too. I sat opposite the woman. I was very nervous, but very happy.

The waiter brought the drinks and the food. We started eating. Then I was very shocked! When the woman talked and laughed, she opened her mouth very wide. I could see all the food inside her mouth! It was terrible!

She laughed very loudly too. I like quiet women, but this woman was very loud. Her friends were loud too. They laughed a lot and they drank a lot. They ordered so many drinks! The woman had around seven cocktails! After two hours, she was very drunk. She laughed more and more.

The next day, my friend called me.

He said, "Do you like her?"

I said, "She is not my type."

The woman was very cute, but I didn't like her way of eating. Also, she drank a lot of alcohol, and she talked and laughed very loudly. I like quiet, elegant women. She was very pretty, but she was not elegant!

I am still looking for a new girlfriend. I hope I can find a nice, quiet girlfriend soon!

THREE

T san (43) Fukuoka Prefecture

I am divorced. I got married when I was twenty-six. My wife was from my hometown. We had a big wedding. When we got married, my wife quit her job. She became a housewife. I was very busy at work every day. I went to work at 7:00am every morning. I usually got home at 11:00pm. A few times a week I went drinking with my co-workers, so I sometimes got home after 12:00 midnight.

My wife cleaned the house and made breakfast and dinner every day. I was very happy. I had a good job and a good wife. However, my wife was not happy. She wanted to talk to me. She wanted to spend time with me. But I was too busy. After two years, she went back to her mother and father's house.

A year later, we got divorced. Of course, I was very upset. Now I am older. I am forty-three. Now, I think at that time, I was bad. I didn't listen to my wife. I didn't spend time with her. That was a mistake.

So now, I am looking for a new wife. It is difficult for me to find a new wife. Now, I am the manager of my office, so I am very busy every day. I also work on Saturdays and sometimes on Sundays.

I live with my mother and father. They are getting old. I am the eldest son, so I have to take care of my mother and father, but it is difficult because I am so busy at work. I need a wife to take care of my mother and father.

Last year, I had two dates. I liked the women, but they didn't like me. I don't know why. Maybe they think I am too old. Or maybe they don't want to take care of my parents. I don't know.

I also joined an Internet dating site. However, I didn't find a good match. I exchanged emails with some women, but we didn't meet. I hope I can find a good wife soon, but I worry I might be single until I die.

FOUR

D san (34) Okayama Prefecture

I had a traditional *o-miai* introduction meeting two years ago. At that time, I was thirty-two. I was working in my family's business. There were only four other employees in the business - my father, my mother, and two men.

I was very busy every day, so I didn't have time to meet women. My parents wanted me to get married. One of my father's friends arranged the *o-miai*. I was not happy. Of course, I wanted to get married, but I wanted to choose my wife by myself. However, my father is very traditional and he is a very proud man. My father's friend is a very rich man. He is a businessman too. The woman was his second daughter. She was twenty-eight at that time. I felt a lot of pressure. I thought, *If I say 'no, I don't want to marry her', her father and my father will be very angry.* So I was very worried and very nervous.

We had the *o-miai* at a very expensive Japanese restaurant. I wore a suit. The woman, Satoko, wore a blue dress. She was very beautiful and elegant. She had very good manners. When I saw her, I became even more nervous. I didn't have the chance to talk to beautiful women very often!

Satoko asked me questions about my job. She was very interested in my work. I relaxed. Her communication skills were very good. I also asked her many questions. She studied Japanese literature at university. We talked about her favorite writers. She was very interesting. After dinner, we had coffee together. We talked more about many things for over an hour.

When I got home, I said to my father, "She is very nice. I want to see her again."

My father was really pleased, and he called Satoko's father.

I was very lucky. Satoko also wanted to see me again!

So, we started dating. We got married six months later. We had a very big wedding in a hotel. Many guests came to the wedding. After the wedding, we went to Europe on our honeymoon.

Now, Satoko lives with my family. She also works in our company. She does office work. We enjoy living and working together. However, very soon, she will stop working. Our baby will be born next year!

At first, I didn't want to have an *o-miai* marriage. I felt a little angry with my father. However, now, I think *o-miai* is a very good system. I found a very good wife. Of course I said "thank you" to my father!

FIVE

A san (34) Tokyo

I am a doctor. Four months ago, I went to a large singles party. I work in a hospital, but I don't want to marry a woman from my hospital. My working life and my private life are separate. At home, I don't want to talk about work.

I was a little nervous before the party. It was my second time to go to a singles party. The first time, I went with my friend. My friend is also a doctor. I don't like parties very much, but I want to get married soon, so I think I have to go to them.

This time, I went alone. All of the men at the party had a high status. They were doctors, company presidents, or graduates from famous Japanese universities, for example, Tokyo University, Kyoto University, or Keio University.

The party was in a large, famous hotel.

All of the women were very beautiful. Many women had very nice hairstyles, and they were wearing a lot of make-up. At the party, I had three minutes of talk time with each woman. Some women were very shy. Others were not shy. They asked me many questions.

There was one woman I liked. Her name was Hiromi. She was twenty-eight. Her hobby was travelling. She went to a foreign country every year. I also enjoy travelling. We talked about travelling for three minutes!

After the talk time, the staff gave us "approach cards." On my approach card, I wrote Hiromi's number. Her number was four. My number was twenty-five. On the approach card I wrote my email address. I was very lucky. She also wanted to meet me!

At the end of the party, the staff announced the couples. The staff announced number four and number twenty-five! After the party, Hiromi and I went to a coffee shop and talked for a few hours.

We talked about travelling and about life. We exchanged phone numbers.

I am very busy every day, so I don't have time to see Hiromi very much, but we email and talk on the phone very often.

I told my mother and father about Hiromi. They were very happy. They want to meet her. My mother said, "Get married soon!"

It is Hiromi's birthday soon. On her birthday, I am going to propose to her.

I hope we can get married soon, and also go on a nice honeymoon. We both like Europe. I would like to go on a honeymoon to Paris. When I propose, I hope Hiromi will say "yes!"

SIX

N san (40) Tokyo

I am a salesman in Tokyo. I had an *o-miai* introduction meeting when I was thirty-six. *O-miai* introduction meetings are not very popular in Japan now, but my mother likes the *o-miai* system. I really don't like *o-miai* meetings. I think they are old style. Modern Japan is different. If I want to get married, I can find a wife by myself. I don't need my mother to arrange it. However, my mother was worried because I was thirty-six and I was still single. So, she arranged an *o-miai* for me.

My family is from Saitama Prefecture, so the *o-miai* meeting was also in Saitama. The woman was the daughter of my mother's friend. She was thirty-two.

Also, at that time, I didn't want to get married. I was enjoying my life in Tokyo. I enjoyed living alone, and seeing my friends after work and on Saturdays and Sundays. Also, I have two older brothers. My eldest brother and his wife live with my mother and father. So, I didn't worry about getting married. My older brother's wife can take care of my parents. However, my mother and father were very worried. They said, "You have to get married soon!"

I didn't want to upset my mother and father, so I went to the *o-miai* meeting. We went to a casual restaurant in my hometown. I introduced myself. The woman didn't look at me. She looked at the table when I was talking. I was surprised. I think eye contact is very important. I am a salesman, so I understand communication very well. I thought, *Maybe she is shy*.

We ordered some food and drinks. I tried to talk to her, but she didn't talk to me. When I asked her questions, she gave me very short answers – "yes", "no", or one word answers.

For example, I asked her, "What do you like doing in your free time?"

She said, "Reading."

I asked, "What kind of books?"

She said, "Manga."

She didn't ask me any questions.

After fifteen minutes, I gave up. I didn't ask her any more questions. She was not interested in me, and I was not interested in her. I didn't want to get married!

When I got home, I said to my mother, "I don't want to see her again. Please don't arrange any more *o-miai* meetings for me! If I want to get married, I will find a nice wife by myself."

My mother and father were not happy. I went back to Tokyo. Now, I am forty. I am still single. But I am happy. Maybe I will never get married. But that is OK for me!

SEVEN

A san (35) Tokyo

I am an office worker in Tokyo. I graduated from Waseda University, and now I work for a famous Japanese company. Many people say, "You work for a large, famous company. You have a good job. You graduated from a famous university. You will find a wife very easily!"

However, I have not found a wife yet. I have been to eight *konkatsu* parties. I like going to *konkatsu* parties. I am not shy, and I like talking. Some parties are big, and some are small. I like them all.

When I get married, I want my wife to stay at home and be a housewife. I don't think married women should work. Women should take care of the house, and family. Also, they should cook and clean well.

When I go to *konkatsu* parties, I always ask the women about their future plans.

I ask, "Do you want to work after you get married?" and "Do you want to stay in Tokyo?"

I also check the women's appearance. Some women wear too much make-up. I don't like that. Also, some women wear too much jewellery. I don't like that either. I think women should wear feminine clothes, but they should look natural. I like the natural style. Some women wear nail art. I really don't like bright nail art!

Last October, I went to a *konkatsu* party in Tokyo. There were about sixty people. The men were all workers in large, famous companies. Some women were very nice. I liked one woman very much. But there was a big problem. She wore too much perfume! I hate perfume.

I asked, "Do you wear perfume every day?"

She said, "Yes, I do. I like perfume very much."

I said, "I'm sorry, I don't like perfume."

She smiled, but she didn't say anything. I think she was a little angry with me.

However, I think direct communication is very important. I have been to many *konkatsu* parties. Many people hide their real feelings. They don't give their straight, honest opinion. I don't like this. Later, if they get married, they will be very unhappy. So, I never hide my true character. I always talk directly. I am still looking for a wife. I am going to a party again next month. I hope I can find a wife at that party!

EIGHT

M san (45) Shimane Prefecture

I met my wife at work fifteen years ago. We worked in a small company. There were only around ten employees. I was an engineer, and she was worked in the office. I was thirty, and she was twenty-five. She was not shy. She talked a lot. She was always smiling and laughing. She had a very big smile. Everyone in the company liked her very much. I enjoyed talking to her. She was very friendly.

At that time, our company had a drinking party once a month. We usually went to an *izakaya*. After that, we sometimes went to a bar or to *karaoke*. Everyone in the company was very friendly and we always had a very good time together.

One evening, after *karaoke*, I asked her, "Would you like to go to a coffee shop for some cake?"

She said, "Yes."

So, we went to a coffee shop. We talked for a long time about many things. We talked about our jobs and our lives. We had a very good time. After that, we went to the coffee shop together many times.

After two years, we got married. When we got married, she quit her job. She became a housewife. Our co-workers were really happy for us. We had a very nice wedding ceremony and wedding party. The president of my company gave a speech. Our first daughter was born a year later. Then, two years after that, our second daughter was born. Now, we have two daughters and we live in a nice house.

Some people say dating co-workers is not good. Some managers don't like office relationships. However, I think it is a very good idea. When we work together, we see the person every day. We can see their good points and their bad points. We can understand them. Also, my wife understands my job. Sometimes I have to work late at night. Sometimes I have to work on Saturdays and Sundays, but my wife is never angry. She knows that sometimes the office is very busy.

There are many ways to meet a marriage partner. Some people go to *konkatsu* parties, some people have *o-miai* meetings, and some people use Internet dating. I have never tried these methods. I met my wife at work fifteen years ago, and we are still very happy together!

THANK YOU

Thank you for reading Men's Konkatsu Tales! We hope you enjoyed it. (Word count: 3,276)

If you enjoyed the book, you might also enjoy the book Women's Konkatsu Tales by I Talk You Talk Press.

If you would like to read more graded readers, please visit our website
http://www.italkyoutalk.com

Other Level 2 graded readers include
Adventure in Rome
Andre's Dream
A Passion for Music
Christmas Tales
Danger in Seattle
Don't Come Back
Finders Keepers...
Marcy's Bakery
Salaryman Secrets!
Stories for Halloween
The Perfect Wedding
The House in the Forest
The School on Bolt Street
Train Travel
Trouble in Paris
Women's Konkatsu Tales

ABOUT THE AUTHOR

I Talk You Talk Press is a Japan-based publisher of language textbooks, graded readers and language learning/teaching resources.

Our team is made up of highly experienced language teachers and translators, who have all studied at least one additional language to an advanced level.

This experience enables us to design our materials from the perspective of both the teacher and the learner. We consult with both teachers and language learners when designing our textbooks and graded readers, and test our materials extensively in the classroom before publication.

We are a fast-growing press, and currently publish graded readers for learners of English. We publish new graded readers monthly.